★ MARCHING ★ FOR FREEDOM

Walk Together, Children, and Don't You Grow Weary

Walk together, children,
Don't you grow weary

Sing together, children,
Don't you grow weary

There's a great camp meeting
in the promised land

—*African American spiritual*
often quoted by Dr. Martin Luther King Jr.

After the marchers' victorious arrival in Montgomery,
Dr. Martin Luther King Jr. addresses the crowd, March 25, 1965.

CONTENTS

Storm clouds gather overhead during the Selma to Montgomery march for the vote, March 1965.

★ MARCHING ★
FOR FREEDOM

Walk Together, Children, and Don't You Grow Weary

Elizabeth Partridge

VIKING

For my dad, Rondal Partridge,
who taught me the power of photography to bear witness.

VIKING
Published by Penguin Group
Penguin Young Readers Group, 345 Hudson Street, New York, New York 10014, U.S.A.
Penguin Group (Canada), 90 Eglinton Avenue East, Suite 700, Toronto, Ontario, Canada M4P 2Y3
(a division of Pearson Penguin Canada Inc.)
Penguin Books Ltd, 80 Strand, London WC2R 0RL, England
Penguin Ireland, 25 St Stephen's Green, Dublin 2, Ireland (a division of Penguin Books Ltd)
Penguin Group (Australia), 250 Camberwell Road, Camberwell, Victoria 3124, Australia
(a division of Pearson Australia Group Pty Ltd)
Penguin Books India Pvt Ltd, 11 Community Centre, Panchsheel Park, New Delhi – 110 017, India
Penguin Group (NZ), 67 Apollo Drive, Rosedale, North Shore 0632, New Zealand
(a division of Pearson New Zealand Ltd.)
Penguin Books (South Africa) (Pty) Ltd, 24 Sturdee Avenue, Rosebank, Johannesburg 2196, South Africa

Penguin Books Ltd, Registered Offices: 80 Strand, London WC2R 0RL, England

First published in 2009 by Viking, a division of Penguin Young Readers Group

1 2 3 4 5 6 7 8 9 10

LIBRARY OF CONGRESS CATALOGING-IN-PUBLICATION DATA
Partridge, Elizabeth.
Marching for freedom : walk together, children, and don't you grow weary / by Elizabeth Partridge.
p. cm.
Includes bibliographical references and index.
ISBN 978-0-670-01189-6 (hardcover)
1. African Americans—Civil rights—Alabama—History—20th century—Juvenile literature. 2.
African American children—Alabama—Political activity—History—20th century—Juvenile literature.
3. Selma to Montgomery Rights March (1965 : Selma, Ala.)—Juvenile literature. 4. Civil rights
movements—Alabama—History—20th century—Juvenile literature. 5. Alabama—Race relations—
History—20th century—Juvenile literature. I. Title.
E185.93.A3P37 2009
323.1196'07307614509041—dc22
2009009696

Manufactured in China   Set in CG Cloister and Matchwood WF   Book design by Jim Hoover

VOTELESS, 1963

THE FIRST TIME Joanne Blackmon was arrested, she was just ten years old. After breakfast one morning, she and her grandmother, Sylvia Johnson, left their apartment in the Carver Homes in Selma, Alabama. Mrs. Johnson walked purposefully down Sylvan Street, turning onto Alabama Street for the six short blocks to the downtown shopping area. Mrs. Johnson intended to register to vote. She knew she wouldn't be allowed to. It was almost impossible for blacks to register. But she wanted to show the white authorities that she, like all Americans, deserved the right to vote.

At the corner of Lauderdale Street they came to the imposing Dallas County Courthouse. Just as they reached the top of the green marble steps, a white lady inside rushed to the glass door and slapped up a sign, CLOSED FOR LUNCH. She threw the lock shut, then stood glaring at them from the other side of the glass.

Joanne's first reaction was surprise: she didn't know white people ate lunch so early. But Mrs. Johnson under-stood immediately what the sign and the woman meant. They weren't welcome.

They didn't head back home, though. The courthouse allowed voter registration only two days a month, and Mrs. Johnson wasn't about to give up so easily. As they stood quietly outside the courthouse they were joined by other applicants, dressed in their Sunday best.

Hours crept slowly by. More people arrived, but the sign didn't come down. No one left the line to go to the bathroom or get a drink of water. Finally, two yellow school buses rumbled up, and the sheriff and his deputies ordered everyone on. Joanne was happy to climb up the deep stairs into the bus. Only white kids got to ride the school bus. She'd never been inside one. It wasn't until they pulled up in front of the city jail that she realized: they were all under arrest.

Over the next two years, Joanne would be jailed ten more times. Her sister Lynda, three years older, would be jailed nine times. They were just two of the hundreds

Samuel Newall stands alone in front of the Dallas County Courthouse with his protest sign, July 8, 1964. Deputies arrested him.

of kids in Selma who met and sang and marched and were jailed over and over again in the struggle for a federal law ensuring every American the right to vote.

After Joanne and Lynda's mother died, their grandmother had moved in with their family. Accustomed to the freedoms up north where she had lived, Mrs. Johnson was angry about how blacks were treated in the South. She urged people to speak up when they were treated unjustly. After moving to Selma, she joined the Dallas County Voters League, a small group led by Amelia Boynton, struggling to get blacks registered. "A vote-less people is a hopeless people," Mrs. Boynton said. Like only a small number of other African Americans, she'd managed to get registered many years earlier. Now, she would prepare people to register, then go with them to the courthouse. All black applicants needed a registered voter to "vouch" that they were a "good Negro." Few registered whites were willing to do it, so Mrs. Boynton would vouch for each person who applied.

Selma, the seat of Dallas County, had a population of 30,000 and was more than half black. But despite Mrs. Boynton's efforts, 99 percent of the voters were white. In nearby Lowndes County, blacks outnumbered whites almost four to one, but not one black had been registered to vote in sixty-five years.

Few dared to even try. The Alabama governor,

Information on applicants was published in the local newspaper to make sure employers and the Ku Klux Klan knew who dared try to register. Applicants were in danger of being fired, losing their homes, or even getting a nighttime visit from the Klan.

George Wallace, made sure it was virtually impossible. He actively promoted use of an unfairly administered "literacy test." Rigged for failure, the test was a series of unreasonable questions about the Constitution and obscure laws. While blacks sat struggling with the test, Mrs. Boynton watched whites walk in, register without being asked to take the test, and walk out ready to vote, without the officially required waiting period. Alabama was also one of five states that required an annual "poll tax," which all voters—black and white—paid each year just for being allowed to vote. To become a registered voter, applicants had to pay the accumulated total of back poll taxes owed for all the years since they were old enough to vote. Poor people simply couldn't afford to vote.

In 1963, Mrs. Boynton was joined by people from the Student Nonviolent Coordinating Committee, SNCC, or "snick." They worked to register voters in Dallas County as well as adjoining counties, but hit huge resistance. Just for talking with Mrs. Boynton or SNCC workers, people could be fired from their jobs, beaten up, or run off the land they sharecropped. By late fall 1964, SNCC workers had only managed to increase the number of black voters in Dallas County from 156 to 335.

Widespread intimidation kept most blacks obeying the rules of segregation, unable to challenge unjust laws and customs. "Fear is the key to it all," said Mrs. Boynton. "Once we lose our fear, we'll be O.K." But how could they make a breakthrough? She strategized with the members of the Dallas County Voters League and came up with a plan. In December, Mrs. Boynton drove to Atlanta. She asked Dr. Martin Luther King Jr. and his

organization, the Southern Christian Leadership Conference, or SCLC, for help. As a leader in the civil rights movement, Dr. King could bring three critical missing components to Selma: motivation, money, and the media.

Mrs. Boynton's timing was perfect. The Civil Rights Act, signed into law on July 2, 1964, by President Lyndon Johnson, had outlawed segregation in schools, workplaces, and public areas such as restaurants and movie theaters. Now removing all barriers to the right to vote had become a top priority for the civil rights movement and SCLC. "If we in the South can win the right to vote," said King, "it will give us the concrete tool with which we ourselves can correct injustice."

King realized Selma had the perfect ingredients for a dramatic protest movement. The racist sheriff, Jim Clark, known for his hair-trigger temper, would stand in stark contrast to demonstrators trained in King's nonviolent philosophy. Alabama's blatantly racist Governor Wallace, with his credo "Segregation now, segregation tomorrow, segregation forever!" was determined to keep blacks from voting. He would undoubtedly thwart every effort to get people registered. Finally, highly motivated civil rights workers were already in Selma and knew the town and its people.

Dr. King didn't waste any time. He decided to kick off the Selma campaign with a speech on January 2, 1965. Rich with symbolism, the date would commemorate Abraham Lincoln's January 1, 1863, signing of the Emancipation Proclamation freeing the slaves. One hundred and two years later it was time for a new kind of freedom.

MARTIN LUTHER KING JR. ARRIVES, 1965

January 2

IT RARELY SNOWED in Selma, but residents of the Carver Homes woke to a light dusting of snow sparkling on the unpaved streets. By early afternoon, people were heading for Brown Chapel African Methodist Episcopal Church, an elegant brick building set squarely in the middle of the Carver Homes.

Singing and clapping soon filled the church and poured out the windows and doors. The crowd swelled, and the singing gathered momentum. Before long, seven hundred people were crammed into the chapel, overflowing the pews and balconies, waiting enthusiastically for Dr. King and the hope he was bringing.

Gathering at Brown Chapel, March 1965.

This little light of mine
I'm going to let it shine
Let it shine, let it shine, let it shine

Like dozens of other children, Joanne and Lynda Blackmon were squeezed into a pew with their family. Now that Lynda was fourteen and old enough to help her father with the three younger kids, their grandmother had moved back home.

Standing silently in the back were two white deputies, noting who had come to the meeting, trying to make them feel vulnerable and exposed.

Dr. King arrived hours late but was greeted with a roar of welcome as he strode up to the altar. His voice washed over the crowd.

Selma, said Dr. King, was a "symbol of bitter-end resistance to the civil rights movement in the Deep South. . . . At the rate they are letting us register now, it will take a hundred and three years to register all of the fifteen thousand Negroes in Dallas County who are qualified to vote. But we don't have that long to wait!"

"Yes, Lord," people shouted.

"We must be ready to march; we must be willing to go to jail by the thousands," Dr. King said. His voice rang out. "Our cry to the state of Alabama is a simple one: give us the ballot!"

"Amen," came the eager response.

"We're not on our knees begging for the ballot," he said. "We are *demanding* the ballot." The crowd jumped to their feet in a standing ovation.

Dr. King would need hundreds of people willing to turn out and protest, in rain and freezing weather. They might be shoved around by armed deputies, jolted with electric cattle prods, chased by men on horseback. They'd need to fill the jails, get bailed out, and go back again. No one—not even Dr. King—could predict what violence and suffering the segregation-loving authorities would unleash to keep blacks from voting. But not one person—no adult, no child—could fight back. Dr. King and his aides promised to teach protesters the principles of nonviolence, the ones Jesus and Gandhi had lived by. These principles had to be adhered to by every person, under any kind of duress, or the movement would fail. A single violent act by a protestor could be used to justify law officers' full use of force, and public sympathy for the protestors would vanish overnight.

Listening to Dr. King preach in the warm, crowded church, Lynda knew right away that she wanted the freedom and dignity he was talking about. It would require, Dr. King said, a steady, loving confrontation. Lynda was willing to do whatever it took. She felt like he was lighting a fire deep in her soul.

Dr. King ended his speech that night promising he'd be back again and again, until they'd made it past every obstacle and the right to vote was theirs.

Dr. King addresses the packed pews at Brown Chapel, January 2, 1965.

January 4–14

A FEW DAYS AFTER hearing Dr. King speak, eight-year-old Sheyann Webb headed out of her Carver Homes apartment for school. She hadn't understood everything Dr. King was talking about, but she had felt his urgency, the importance of his message, the full-throated, joyful response he was given by the congregation.

Instead of crossing the street toward school, she lingered on the corner watching black and white people standing together, talking. She could tell something was in the air. When the people went inside the church, she slipped in behind them.

King had gone back to Atlanta for a few weeks, but there were forty or fifty people inside listening to one of his aides, Hosea Williams, a firebrand who always pushed for action.

Sheyann sat quietly in a pew listening to Williams explain the importance of the right to vote. The vote would mean freedom—freedom to vote for just laws, freedom to elect judges and mayors and governors who would make sure the laws were enforced. One of Williams's phrases rang in Sheyann's mind: "If you can't vote," he said, "you're a slave." Sheyann was mesmerized. When they broke for lunch she suddenly realized the morning was gone, and ran to school.

Excitement gathered around the SCLC and SNCC workers. Even what they called themselves—Freedom Fighters—felt promising. Some days Sheyann cut school and sat in the back of the church listening. When she went to school, her teachers would ask her what was going on in the church. What were the Freedom Fighters saying? Teachers were afraid to go to the meetings. The all-white school board would fire them if they went.

After school let out for the day, Sheyann would meet up with her best friend, Rachel West, who lived next door. Rachel's parents had opened their apartment to take in King's aides from out of town. James Bevel, an impassioned, visionary aide to King, was staying with them. He said gaining the right to vote was more important than anything they'd done before: it could open all the doors that were still shut tight.

The Freedom Fighters made a point of reaching out to teenagers, wanting to get them involved. To make the movement in Selma succeed, they'd need the full-on participation of people too young to vote. In the Birmingham civil rights protests in 1963, when there had no longer been enough adults willing to fill the jails, kids and young adults had stepped up. Being blasted by high-powered fire hoses hadn't stopped them, nor had being attacked by snarling police dogs. As young as six, they'd stood their ground until arrested, then gone to

jail proudly, to the dismay of their terrified parents.

"Don't worry about your children," Dr. King had reassured parents. "Don't hold them back if they want to go to jail." He was in awe of their willingness and bravery. "They are doing a job for not only themselves but for all of America and for all mankind. They are carving a tunnel of hope through the great mountain of despair." Kids were so integral to the success of the Birmingham struggle that it had quickly become known as the "Children's Crusade."

Rachel West and Sheyann Webb listen to speakers in Brown Chapel.

Now it was time for the students in Selma to step up. First, they had to learn to question the way they lived. "Why do you have to drink out of the 'colored' fountain?" the Freedom Fighters asked them. "Why can't your mother and father vote?"

Charles Mauldin, a quiet, serious student at the all-black Hudson High in Selma, was intrigued. "I always had an answer for everything and I was really stunned because I had no answer for those questions." There were so many aspects of segregation he had blindly followed. Why did he have to step off the sidewalk when a white person walked by? Why wasn't he allowed to look whites directly in the face?

Charles remembered when he was eleven or twelve, hiding under someone's front porch on Jefferson Davis Avenue, watching a long line of cars full of hooded Ku Klux Klan members drive openly, arrogantly, through his all-black neighborhood. It had seemed to Charles that more than a hundred cars rolled by. He realized he could be taken away by men in hoods, and nobody could stop them. What made it especially sickening was that he probably knew many of them from his job as a caddy at Selma's all-white country club.

At first Charles was intimidated by what it would take to challenge the way things were in Selma. But he started going to meetings, listening to the Freedom Fighters. Nonviolence did not mean being passive. Students had to be willing to march in the streets and face off against the deputies so their parents could stand in line to register.

Since they weren't the breadwinners, teens and children could afford to go to jail repeatedly without jeopardizing the family's income. The movement needed people to take dramatic risks to challenge unjust laws. Were the students willing?

Charles and other students were eager to accept the challenge, but one thing was nearly impossible to understand: How could they let someone spit on them, beat them, or hurt them, and not fight back?

Freedom Fighters explained they were already taking all kinds of hurt, being injured every single day. Violence was more than physical blows to the body: it was psychological blows to the mind and spirit as well. And did they react violently? No, they stepped off the sidewalk, kept their heads down. They did only what whites allowed them to do. Now it was time to stand up for their rights, for a sense of purpose and dignity, and to do it without any violence. They weren't trying to dominate, or be the winner—they were trying to change their relationship with whites so they could be equal partners as Americans.

Charles spread the word. He encouraged others at his high school to come to meetings of the Dallas County Youth League in the basement of Tabernacle Baptist Church. With his steady, thoughtful ways, Charles was elected the group's leader.

Bobby Simmons, another student at Hudson High, was skeptical that they could change their relationship with whites. "From a child up at that time you was taught to fear them," he said. "Our parents explained

---

Young convicts at work in the field in 1903. Boys and men were often shackled in heavy chains as they worked.

to us kids that the white was almost the Great God or the Great Father. If they say we couldn't go places, we couldn't go." The Silver Moon Café, the Garden Café, Thirsty Boy Drive-In—all were off limits. Even after the Civil Rights Act outlawed segregation, the owner of Carter's drugstore had hit a boy in the head with an ax handle when he'd sat down at the lunch counter. Bobby understood why parents insisted on obeying the rules. "They had a lot of fear in them," he said, "because

of the punishment they had took and the abuse."

Bobby's mother was hysterical. She thought they would all end up getting killed. She was terrified Bobby would be jailed. "Please," she begged him, "leave that mess alone." She was old enough to remember when conditions for jailed blacks were horrific. Up until World War II twenty-five years earlier, men—even teenagers and younger—could be snatched off the streets, thrown in jail on the flimsiest of charges such as vagrancy, using

obscene language, or gambling. After being sentenced, they'd quickly be sold by the deputies in a convict leasing program—*sold* as laborers to plantations, lumber mills, turpentine camps, mines, and factories throughout the Deep South until they had worked off their jail time. Shackled, fed poorly, worked hard, and cruelly punished, many convicts died.

Bobby didn't want to upset his mother. But something new was happening now, exhilarating and empowering. He would slip away from the house, not telling her where he was going.

The students began their meetings singing spirituals, gospel, and freedom songs—new lyrics put to comforting songs everyone already knew. Someone would "raise" a song—starting it up with a verse, and the others would join in. Their voices blended into a rich sound as they poured their commitment into the song.

Lynda made it to nearly every youth league meeting. She could feel that something really big was going to happen. "The movement was like a fire inside that just kept spreading and spreading and spreading," she said. "It was not a fire that you wanted to put out. It was something that you wanted to increase and let burn." Every morning she woke up singing freedom songs.

Joanne was the youngest to regularly attend the student meetings, and became the group go-fer. She didn't mind. The talks at the meetings sometimes bored her so much she was happy to run errands. But where words failed, the singing reached deep inside her, filling her with the spirit of the movement.

Blacks and whites were not allowed to use the same restrooms. Segregation laws even extended to vending machines.

January 18–22

MONDAY, JANUARY 18, Dr. King returned to Selma and led an inspiring rally at Brown Chapel. The next day the courthouse would be open for voter registration, and he would march there with willing people. After his speech, Sheyann and Rachel were invited up to sing in front of the congregation.

Rachel got home to find her apartment jammed with people. Besides her seven brothers and sisters, Freedom Fighters filled the apartment, sitting on the couch, the chairs, even the floor. Rachel was excited and a little frightened. While her mother made cup after cup of instant coffee, they talked about the days to come. Rachel lay on the living room floor and listened. Right in her apartment were whites and blacks, Catholics and

Baptists, all willing to put their lives on the line for one thing: freedom. That night, she fell asleep thinking this wasn't just King's movement or the people's movement. It was something greater, something divine.

The next day was sunny but cold. Three hundred children and adults gathered in Brown Chapel and headed out. Sheyann walked with the one teacher in her school who dared to march, Mrs. Margaret Moore. They passed city hall on Alabama Street and headed to the courthouse.

While everyone waited outside, Mrs. Boynton took an old black farmer into the courthouse to register. He nervously began to fill out the form. The registrar, looking at his writing, said, "Now, you're going across the line, old man. You failed already, you can't register, you can't vote, you just as well get out of line."

The old man straightened up and looked right at the registrar. "Mr. White Man," he said, "you can't tell me that I can't register. I'll try anyway. For I own a hundred and forty acres of land. I've got ten children who are grown and many of them are in a field where they can help other people. I took these hands that I have and made crops to put them through school. If I am not worthy of being a registered voter, then God have mercy on this city."

Mrs. Boynton stepped back. She figured he had said it all. She left the courthouse and began to walk down the sidewalk. Sheriff Clark ordered her to join the line of people waiting to register. She refused and kept walking. There was no reason for her to be in line. Clark hated to be disobeyed. He lost his temper, pushed her roughly down the sidewalk into a patrol car, and arrested her.

The sheriff began shouting at the marchers. People jammed tightly together as deputies with nightsticks and electric cattle prods closed in on them. Sheyann wanted to run. "Baby, don't be afraid," said Mrs. Moore. "You're young, but just don't be afraid."

Deputies herded them down Alabama Street toward city hall, shoving the marchers with their clubs and jolting them with the cattle prods.

More than sixty people were arrested, but Sheyann was able to slip away as the marchers were herded up to the second floor of city hall to the jail, to be held under "charges named later."

The metal door clanged shut behind the marchers. It was frightening to be jailed, to hear the scrape of the key in the lock. But they were together. Humming, swaying, shoulders touching shoulders, they found their way into one freedom song, then another.

The next day a photograph of Mrs. Boynton's arrest was carried by *The New York Times* and *The Washington Post*. Footage of her arrest dominated television newscasts. Across the United States, people were shocked by the sheriff's rough treatment. Suddenly Selma had the national attention Dr. King sought.

Students cut school and held an impassioned meeting. Thanks to the Freedom Fighters, they'd learned to look at their lives very differently. As long as they were forced to live within strict limits imposed by violence and humiliation, they were still slaves. That had to change. "If *death* was the option to not being a slave," said one student, Charles Bonner, "then so be it."

Oh freedom
Oh freedom
Oh freedom over me!
And before I'll be a slave
I'll be buried in my grave
And go home to my Lord and be free

These were powerful words, put to deeply rhythmic music more than a century earlier by enslaved blacks. "That song was always very motivating to us," said Charles. "We sang it with great passion."

LEFT: *Charles Bonner explains to newsmen why he is protesting. Sheriff Clark looks on.* RIGHT: *Sheriff Clark sticks his billy club in a man's neck as he orders waiting applicants to move away from the Dallas Courthouse. In the same hand, Clark holds an electric cattle prod.*

Still singing, the students marched to the courthouse. "Not that any of us were so brave we weren't scared," said Charles. "We were scared to death. We acted in spite of the fear."

The sheriff arrested as many of them as he could. They were bused to the county work farm, overfilling the long, narrow buildings. Each building had only one metal toilet, one sink. People shared blankets, and once the bunks were filled, slept on the filthy floor. They were fed black-eyed peas, undercooked and gritty with sand. Sometimes they had plain grits with no salt or butter, or a boiled chicken neck. Deputies hid behind doors and jolted them with cattle prods as they went through. "They treated you miserable," said Bobby.

But no one had to stay in jail long. Lawyers, using money from the SCLC coffers, worked around the clock posting bail, getting people out as fast as they could. "After the first time you go to jail," Bobby said, "you get the fear out of you." He'd keep marching.

Outraged by the students' arrests, the black teachers had finally had enough—their students were showing more courage than they were. They met in the high school cafeteria and decided to march to the courthouse on Friday afternoon, January 22. One hundred and five teachers—nearly every member of the Selma Negro Teachers Association—decided: it was time to get registered or go to jail trying.

But Clark refused to even admit them to the court-house. Looming above them on the stairs, fuming, he accused the teachers of making a mockery of the court-house. Decades of training made it hard to look right at the burly sheriff as he lectured them. Their eyes flitted up to his face, then darted back down. But they stood their ground. Reporters lounged across the street, waiting for some action.

The white superintendent showed up and told the teachers to leave. They stayed. The superintendent conferred with Clark, insisting he hold back and make no arrests. It would be a disaster if Clark jailed the teachers, or if he had them all fired. Nearly every black kid in Selma would be on the loose, free to join the protests. After being shoved and prodded backward by the deputies, the teachers realized they weren't going to be jailed, and they marched to Brown Chapel.

Students were waiting in three churches. They'd agreed to pack the jails if their teachers weren't allowed to register. When the teachers solemnly walked in to Brown Chapel, everyone leaped up, applauding. Kids danced around, hugging and congratulating them. It was unbelievable that the teachers had defied Sheriff Clark and the superintendent. Never before had a group of black teachers marched together in the civil rights struggle in the Deep South. From Brown Chapel, they called the other two churches. All the students headed out, straight into the waiting arms of the deputies.

RIGHT: *Teens often spent hours in church, singing, chanting, listening to speeches, and waiting. Some would leave the church to protest in the morning, and after they'd been arrested, a second group would head out.*

February 1–17

ON MONDAY, FEBRUARY 1, Dr. King told an assembly at Brown Chapel that more than seven hundred people were gathered to march in nearby Perry County, expanding the movement. In another church in Selma, students were preparing to take off on their own march. "Even though they cannot vote," King thundered, "they are determined to be freed through their parents." He led 260 demonstrators out of Brown Chapel in a cold, drizzling rain. They headed up the street in a burst of freedom songs.

We're gonna do what the spirit say do
We're gonna do what the spirit say do
What the spirit say do we're gonna
*   do, oh Lord*
We're gonna do what the spirit say do

They were all promptly arrested, including King and his trusted aide, Ralph Abernathy. They refused to be bailed out. The day after their arrest, Charles Mauldin led more than three hundred students to the courthouse. "We

want to make them arrest us," he said. "We'll lock arms in front of the courthouse." They sang freedom songs until Sheriff Clark yelled, "All of you underage are under arrest for truancy and the others for contempt of court. Turn that line around and let's go."

They were marched down to the old armory, a huge hangar with a cement floor. After processing the students at tables set up at one end of the building, deputies forced the boys to face the wall and stand on their tiptoes, their hands high up on the wall. The deputies paced behind the boys, reciting with relish what they'd do to them next: hang them from trees or drag them to death behind their cars. But the threats were empty. There were far too many reporters in town watching every move they made. The deputies settled for leaving everyone to spend the night on the cold floor.

Twelve-year-old Martha Griffin, a sixth grader, was one of the jailed students. "We had to sleep on the cement, with no cover," she said. "And all those *things* [the guards] around there!"

Would she march again? "I'll be right there," she said. "I ain't scared of those old things. They stuck my sister in the head with a pole and everything, but I'm not scared of them."

Across the United States, people were shocked that Dr. King encouraged children to join in the civil rights struggle. "A hundred times I have been asked," he said, "why we have allowed children to march in demonstrations, to freeze and suffer in jails, to be exposed to bul-

lets and dynamite. The answer is simple. Our children and our families are maimed a little every day of our lives. If we can end an incessant torture by a single climactic confrontation, the risks are acceptable."

On February 5, more than nine hundred students poured out of school to protest. In an effort to keep the kids off the streets, the all-white school board instituted a demerit system, threatening to expel kids who missed school, and warned parents they could be charged with misdemeanors if their children weren't in class.

But the marches didn't stop. Neither did the arrests. Prisoners were moved out of the surrounding jails as demonstrating adults and kids were crammed in.

The students kept their spirits up with their own lyrics to the civil rights song "If You Miss Me from the Back of the Bus."

If you miss Governor Wallace
You can't find him nowhere
Just come on over to the crazy house
He'll be resting over there

If you miss Jim Clark
You can't find him nowhere
Just come on over to the graveyard
He'll be lying over there

After one arrest, Lynda spent eight days on a prison farm. But as soon as she was bailed out, she marched

---

A policeman escorts teen marchers to jail following a demonstration in front of the courthouse, Selma 1965.

again. Sometimes jailors would wait until the middle of the night, then open the gates and tell the kids to go. From the Selma Prison Camp, it was several cold, dark miles to walk home, with no way to let their parents know where they were. They just prayed there was no one waiting in the dark to ambush them.

Sheriff Clark, frustrated he hadn't stopped the marches, was increasingly agitated. On February 10, Charles marched with a group of students to the front of the courthouse. Arms linked, they stood singing in front of Clark and his deputies.

Instead of herding them off to jail as the students expected, Clark and his deputies brought around their squad cars and chased the students several miles out into the countryside. The deputies took turns jumping out of their cars, hitting and jabbing at them with nightsticks and cattle prods to keep them going. "You've been wanting to march," the deputies shouted. "Now let's go!"

"God sees you," a fifteen-year-old said to a deputy, who clubbed him across the mouth. The students limped back into town, shaken and tearful, throwing up with exhaustion and fear.

Thirteen-year-old Cliff Moton was on the forced march. It made him mad to be run like that. But he'd kept going. "You'd be beat if you didn't," he said. He'd been jailed earlier, but he was going to keep marching. "I want my parents to be able to get better jobs," he said. "When I grow up, I want to be a carpenter. And be able to vote. I want my children not to have to be in this mess like we are in now."

At first his mother didn't want him to protest, afraid she'd lose her job. The day he got out of jail, she didn't say anything to him. But by the next morning, she told him it was all right. Go on, she said.

Charles refused to let the forced march stop him. "You have to cut yourself off from your feelings," he said. "You didn't let yourself think about it or you would quit. We'd simply go back to the church and plan the next day." He kept going, organizing, encouraging, leading groups of teenagers and kids out of the church to protest. "I'm proud of you," he said to all of them after one march. "I used to wish I was white. Now I wish I was blacker."

Watching their kids, more parents began to come to the meetings and join the marches, despite the risks. "The adults that came out anyway knew that their livelihoods were in danger, that they could be hung, killed in some horrible way—disappear forever, and their families would be left without any help," said Joanne. "But yet they still got up and did it."

If you cannot sing a congregational song at full power, you cannot fight in any struggle. . . . It is something you learn.

In congregational singing you don't sing a song—you raise it. By offering the first line, the song leader just offers the possibility, and it is up to you, individually, whether you pick it up or not. . . . It is a big personal risk because you will put everything into the song. It is like stepping off into space. A mini-

*revolution takes place inside of you. Your
body gets flushed, you tremble, you're tempted
to turn off the circuits. But that's when you
have to turn up the burner and commit yourself to follow that song wherever it leads.
This transformation in yourself that you
create is exactly what happens when you join
a movement. You are taking a risk—you are
committing yourself and there is no turning
back.*

*When you get together at a mass meeting
you sing the songs which symbolize transformation, which make that revolution of courage
inside you. . . . You raise a freedom song.*

—*Bernice Johnson Reagon,
singer, songwriter, Freedom Fighter*

Marches and arrests continued nearly every single
day. At one point, Lynda was one of twenty-three girls
crammed into a cell meant for two people in the city jail.
The mattresses had been taken out, and the girls slept
on the floor or the iron bed frames. By the third day, one
girl was sick. Despite their pleas to the deputies for help,
the girls were given brooms and told to clean the cell.
Lynda grabbed hold of the broom handle, smashed out
the small window overlooking Franklin Street, a black
shopping area, and yelled for help.

The furious deputies rushed in. They made some
ugly remarks, then herded all the girls into a sweat box—
a small metal cell with no windows. When the door
clanged shut behind them, it was pitch black. They were
packed in so tightly no one could move. It quickly became stifling hot and humid, filled with their own stale,
exhaled air. The dark, crowded box was terrifying. How
long would they be left inside? Would they run out of air
and suffocate to death? Lynda passed out.

When she came to, jail inmates were carrying her
and the other girls into the courtroom. She had no idea
how long they'd been left in the sweat box. The judge
told them all to write down their names and go home.
"And for God's sake," he said as they left, "bathe!"

Hudson High students sing at a meeting.

February 19–March 6

NERVES WERE INCREASINGLY frayed on both sides. Whites were tired of the constant marches, the "outside agitators," and reporters in town. Freedom Fighters were dismayed that they'd made no significant progress, despite more than three thousand arrests. They decided to ratchet up the intensity of the demonstrations with a march in Marion, a town thirty miles northwest of Selma. This time it would be a night march, much more dangerous because of what could happen under the cover of darkness. Leaders knew it was risky, but night marches forced into public view the lawlessness always lurking below the surface.

At 9:30 P.M. on February 19, four hundred and fifty people set out from the tiny Zion Methodist Church in Marion. Whites rushed out from nowhere, smashing cameras and spraying black paint across TV camera lenses. Suddenly the streetlights were cut off. Police and state troopers stormed the marchers, swinging their nightsticks across shoulders, into vulnerable stomachs and skulls. The dark street filled with screams and shouts as the panicked marchers fled for safety.

Some people ran back to the church, others into any place they could find shelter from the flailing, cracking sticks. Eighty-two-year-old Cager Lee was hit in the head and ran, bleeding, into Mack's Café.

Troopers rushed in after him, nightsticks swinging. Lee's daughter and his grandson Jimmie Lee Jackson tried to protect him. Jackson was slammed against a cigarette machine and shot twice in the stomach by a state trooper. He staggered out the door and fell to the ground, where he lay unconscious and bleeding. More than three hours later he was finally taken to the hospital.

To protest the brutality in Marion, Selma students decided to hold a night march of their own. One hundred kids and teenagers gathered on February 23 at Brown Chapel. Waiting until the sun was low in the sky, they headed for the courthouse, trailed by reporters. A few blocks from the chapel, they were stopped by James Baker, Selma's Commissioner of Public Safety. A moderate man, he didn't want the students to reach the courthouse because he knew the forces gathered there: Sheriff Clark was lying in wait, along with his deputies, posse members, and seventy-five state troopers who'd been in Marion.

Baker raised his bullhorn and warned the oncoming marchers, in the interest of their own safety, to turn around. They knelt in prayer. A few minutes later, he diplomatically asked them to go peacefully back to their church. Quietly at first, then bursting into song, the students walked back the way they'd come. Just being out together at twilight, they'd publicly shown their defiance. As the sun set in a blaze of orange, the students were safely back in the church.

On February 25, Jimmie Lee Jackson died from his wounds. James Bevel, the brilliant, stormy preacher staying with Rachel's family, was distraught over his death.

He met with Jackson's mother and his bandaged grandfather, who swore he was ready to march again right away. Bevel was used to the tremendous courage shown in the face of violence, but Jackson's death hit him hard.

In the pulpit at Brown Chapel that Sunday, Bevel was lit up with anger and bitterness. He said he wanted to take Jackson's body all the way to Montgomery and lay it on the state capitol steps where Governor Wallace worked. He wanted the governor to see the lethal violence he sanctioned.

It was a crazy, grief-inspired idea. When Bevel calmed down, he realized that Jimmie Lee Jackson needed to be buried. But he also had a new idea. Speaking to a crowd of more than six hundred at Brown Chapel, he called on the congregation to march all the way to Montgomery, more than fifty miles away. "Be prepared to walk to Montgomery!" he shouted from the pulpit. "Be prepared to sleep on the highway!"

The idea caught on like wildfire. On March 3, Dr. King presided at Jackson's funeral in Marion. More than a thousand mourners came to honor Jackson. They crushed into the tiny church, and stood outside in a light rain. After the service, they walked three miles behind Jackson's casket in a cold, drenching rain to lay him to rest in Heard Cemetery. Dr. King announced that a march from Selma to Montgomery would take place the following Sunday, March 7.

A man speaks into a megaphone at a night march in Selma, March 1965.

Marchers walk through downtown Selma, March 7, 1965, led by John Lewis, far right, and Hosea Williams,
next to him. Sixth from the right, with his hands in his pockets, is Charles Mauldin.

BLOODY SUNDAY

March 7, 1965

BY NOON ON March 7, hundreds were milling around Brown Chapel, waiting for the march to start. Rumors flew that the troopers would use tear gas on them. "Tear gas will not keep you from breathing," a doctor explained. "You may feel like you can't breathe for awhile. Tear gas will not make you permanently blind. It may blind you temporarily. Do not rub your eyes."

Charles Mauldin reviewed protective moves with a group of kids and teenagers. Dodge any blows you could. If clubbed or kicked, curl into a tight ball and protect your stomach. If tear-gassed, drop to the ground to breathe, as the gas would slowly rise.

Rachel practiced with the others. She put her nose to the ground to breathe over and over again, with a growing sense of alarm. She couldn't stop thinking about all the ways they could be hurt. Snipers could hide behind trees. Clark's posse, on their huge horses, with their clubs and cattle prods, could chase them down. Bombs could be hidden in the church when they gathered, or flung through the windows.

Everyone was tense. Clark had put out a call for more deputies, and Governor Wallace had made it clear that he would stop the march. No doubt people would be jailed; some might even be injured. Dr. King was not there to reassure and inspire the marchers. Because of recent death threats, his advisors had talked him into staying away. He was in Atlanta, preaching at the church he co-pastored with his father.

The marchers set off around four in the afternoon, led by Freedom Fighters Hosea Williams and John Lewis. In case of trouble, another Freedom Fighter, Andrew Young, stayed behind at Brown Chapel. The marchers walked two by two down Sylvan Street, turned right onto Water Street, and headed for the bridge. No one sang or clapped. No one even talked. There was just the sound of their scuffling feet on the pavement. Mrs. Boynton and Charles were close behind Williams and Lewis. Not far behind them were Lynda, Bobby, and Sheyann. Lynda wanted her sister beside her, but Joanne lingered at the church, then joined the line farther back with friends. Rachel stood in front of Brown Chapel, watching the marchers leave, too afraid to join. Everyone was quiet, solemn, and anxious. What lay ahead?

A left turn took the marchers onto the Edmund

Pettus Bridge, arching high up over the Alabama River, too steep for the marchers to see the other side. When Williams and Lewis hit the crest of the bridge, they came to a dead stop.

At the foot of the bridge stood a line of Alabama State Troopers in blue uniforms and helmets, blocking the road. To one side was Sheriff Clark's posse, sitting high on their horses. White bystanders waited on the frontage road, shouting and jeering.

Williams and Lewis stepped forward, and the march resumed. "We were going to get killed or we were going to get free," said one marcher.

Looking straight ahead, Charles didn't let himself think about how vulnerable he felt. He had set his mind on Montgomery. "There's a type of coolness that you develop, a steeling of the nerves so that you can accept whatever happens," he explained. "There was no going back, and so you're willing to accept whatever it takes. That's what we were equipped with, just a sense of moral indignity."

Troopers and posse pulled on gas masks, felt for the nightsticks hanging from their belts. Williams and Lewis walked to within fifty feet of the troopers and stopped. They were ordered to disperse in the next two minutes. "Go home or go to your church," said a trooper through a bullhorn.

They stood.

One minute and five seconds later, troopers shoved into the marchers, swinging their clubs. Whites watching from the sidelines whooped and cheered. Charles heard John Lewis's head crack as a billy club hit him. Lewis threw up an arm to protect himself, was struck again, and fell to the pavement.

Tear gas canisters crashed onto the bridge, spewing thick clouds of gas. Lewis felt strangely calm as he lay on the pavement. "This is it," he thought. "People are going to die here. *I'm* going to die here." Mrs. Boynton was struck in the head, blacked out, and fell to the ground.

Charles's lungs were imploding from the tear gas. Desperate for air, he ran to a low area near the river where tear gas hovered a few feet about the ground. But a mounted posse forced him back to the bridge, into the gas. Bobby dodged the troopers, ran forward, and was cut off from the bridge, caught in the parking strip in front of several small businesses. "People were laying out, bleeding, coughing, crying," he said. "We were pure defenseless."

Lynda, still on the bridge, was enveloped in clouds of

LEFT: Moments before the Alabama State Troopers attack, white onlookers eager to watch gather on the sidelines. Charles Mauldin is at the right under the Coca-Cola sign. ABOVE: A burly trooper swings his billy club at John Lewis's head. The blow left him hospitalized.

tear gas. A trooper grabbed her from behind, one hand at the back of her collar and one in front, and pulled her backward. Without thinking, she bit the hand in front, hard, and was hit over her eye with a billy club. The hands pushed her forward, and she was hit again on the back of her head. She stood and ran, chased deeper into the tear gas by the trooper.

The posse urged their horses forward into the running, falling, screaming marchers. Sheyann ran blindly back up the steep slope of the bridge, afraid she'd tumble off the bridge into the water or be trampled to death. Suddenly a Freedom Fighter scooped her up under the armpits and kept running up the bridge. Legs pumping, she yelled at him to put her down. He was running too slowly. But he held on tight until they were across the bridge before he let her go.

The waves of tear gas hit Joanne, still on the upslope of the bridge. People were running past her, screaming, followed by state troopers swinging their billy clubs. Even the horses, surrounded by terrified people, breathing tear gas themselves, were frightened. "They ran those horses up into the crowd and were knocking people down, horses rearing up, kicking people," she said. "Blood was everywhere." Joanne saw a dazed woman step in front of a horse and get knocked to the ground, her head bouncing on the pavement. Joanne fainted.

Panicked marchers ran back to the Carver Homes, chased by the posse, who were beating and whipping any

Wearing gas masks, troopers use their billy clubs to force protestors back into the choking, blinding cloud of tear gas.

marchers they could reach. "They would lean over the horse and hit you as hard as they could," said Bobby. "It was so cruel." He made it back across the bridge, dodging uniformed Selma firemen who were grabbing people and holding them for the posse to hit.

When Joanne groggily came to, she was lying in the back of a car parked beside the bridge. Lynda was bending over her, crying and crying, her tears dropping down on Joanne. When Joanne came fully awake, she realized it wasn't tears but blood from two gashes in Lynda's head dripping on her.

Lynda was taken to the hospital, where doctors and nurses worked feverishly to care for more than one hundred patients laid out on every surface, even the floor of the employees' dining room. Around her, people's bloody lacerations were stitched shut, broken bones were set, and tear gas washed out of irritated, burning eyes. It took more than thirty stitches to close Lynda's wounds, but the pain was nothing compared to the searing realization she had about the white men who'd attacked them. "It was pure hatred," she said. "They came ready to do what they did. They would go to any means necessary to keep us subservient and docile. These people beating us, they took pleasure in it."

As battered, coughing children staggered home, furious fathers grabbed their guns. Charles's mother stopped her husband as he tried to get out the door. At Brown Chapel, Andrew Young had to talk sense into men who wanted to fight back. The .32 or .38 shotguns they had were no match for automatic rifles and ten-gauge shotguns. There were at least two hundred guns out there filled with buckshot. "You ever see what buckshot does

to a deer?" Young asked. Most of them had. They realized it would be suicidal to try to fight back.

That evening, everyone crept into Brown Chapel. The smell of tear gas, clinging to people's clothes and hair, hung heavily in the room. Sheyann came in the back door and stood and looked at everyone for a long time before she sat down. It wasn't that people were afraid: it was as if they didn't care to try any longer. The hope had been beaten out of them. It was, she said, "like we were slaves after all and had been put in our place by a good beating."

Some people sat in stunned silence; some were crying and softly moaning. After a while, a slow, quiet humming mixed in with the moaning. At first it wasn't clear what the song was, it was so slow, like the sound of a funeral song. Then the humming and moaning got louder, and picked up speed.

> *Ain't gonna let nobody, Lordy, turn*
> * me 'round . . .*
> *Turn me 'round . . .*
> *Turn me 'round . . .*
> *Ain't gonna let nobody, Lordy, turn*
> * me 'round . . .*
> *Keep on a-walkin'*
> *Keep on a-talkin'*
> *Marching up to Freedom land.*

Soon the song was coming out loud and strong and pure. New verses were made up as they sang. Ain't gonna let no horses turn me 'round . . . no tear gas . . . no sheriff . . . no troopers. . . . People leaped to their feet, clapping and swaying, singing some more. They took their defeat and sang their way back to strength. They'd stayed committed to nonviolence. They were willing to go out again and face state troopers and mounted posses with whips and tear gas and clubs. The music made them bigger than their defeat, bigger than their fear. It wove them together, filled them once more with courage and strength.

While the marchers were in the church, footage taken by news crews was being broadcast across the country on all three major television networks. ABC interrupted a Nazi war crimes movie, *Judgment at Nuremberg*, to show viewers the violence in Selma. People were shocked to see composed, nonviolent Americans being attacked by heavily armed troopers on horses. ABC let the footage run for nearly fifteen minutes. Forty-eight million viewers watched in growing disbelief and horror as men, women, and children desperately fled for safety.

In Atlanta, Dr. King was distraught that he hadn't been with the marchers. He immediately sent telegrams to more than two hundred religious leaders sympathetic to the civil rights movement, asking them to come to Selma for a peaceful march on Tuesday.

A woman tends to Amelia Boynton, who lies unconscious on the ground at left.

TURN AROUND TUESDAY

March 9

A THOUSAND EAGER, anxious people crammed into Brown Chapel Monday night for a mass meeting. Clergy had been arriving all day and sat in the front pews. At 10:30 Dr. King finally arrived. The crowd leaped to its feet and burst into song:

> *Mine eyes have seen the glory of the*
> *coming of the Lord:*
> *He is trampling out the vintage where*
> *the grapes of wrath are stored;*
> *He hath loosed the fateful lightning*
> *of His terrible swift sword:*
> *His truth is marching on.*

For nearly five minutes they sang and clapped before settling down to let Dr. King speak. Grateful to the newly arrived clergy, he asked them to stand and introduce themselves. They were Catholic and Protestant, Baptist and Jewish. There were priests and nuns, pastors and rabbis. This was bigger than any difference in worship: this was a time for all to respond to Dr. King's call.

"Thank God we're not alone," Dr. King said to each of them after they introduced themselves. He gave a heartfelt tribute to the marchers who had endured beatings and tear gas, then he roused the crowd for Tuesday's march. "We must let them know that if they beat one Negro they are going to have to beat a hundred," he thundered, "and if they beat a hundred, then they are going to have to beat a thousand."

Late that night Dr. King was told that a federal judge was issuing a court order prohibiting the march until further notice. The order put Dr. King in a terrible bind. He had no qualms about violating state and local laws that were rigged against blacks, but this was different. In all his civil disobedience he'd never defied a federal order. He was counting on the federal courts to uphold civil rights legislation.

Informed of the court order, President Johnson was adamant that Dr. King needed to wait. Marching now, in defiance of the order, could be used to justify renewed violence from Governor Wallace's state troopers. Aides for the president worked deep into the night, phoning and visiting King, asking him to reconsider. President Johnson even had his Attorney General call Dr. King, begging

him to be patient and postpone the march until there was a hearing. Dr. King listened thoughtfully, then replied, "Mr. Attorney General, you have not been a black man in America for the past three hundred years."

King arrived at Brown Chapel Tuesday morning with a heavy heart, unsure what to do. More than two thousand people crowded around the chapel, including most of Hudson High's students. The mood was incredibly tense as everyone readied themselves for a repeat of the violence of Bloody Sunday. But they weren't going to back down: the time for justice was this day, this moment.

King disappeared into the parsonage of Brown Chapel to strategize and pray with his aides. People milled around the grounds of Carver Homes, waiting. At two o'clock, Dr. King emerged and stood on the stairs of the chapel. The crowd moved in closer to listen. "I do not know what lies ahead of us." King's voice rolled across the crowd. "There may be beatings, jailings, tear gas. But I would rather die on the highways of Alabama than make a butchery of my soul."

Joanne was afraid to go, but she got in line close to the front with Lynda. "I held Lynda's hand this time," Joanne

Despite the cold weather, people waited outside on the grounds of the Carver Homes to hear Dr. King speak, March 9, 1965.

said. "She didn't have to worry about me bein' anywhere else but with her." Despite his own deep misgivings, their father had encouraged them to march. "If you don't go," he said, "it means they won." Bobby, Charles, and Sheyann all joined the march as it left Brown Chapel.

By 2:30, Dr. King was leading the marchers up the arch of the Edmund Pettus Bridge and down the other side, where he was ordered to halt. One hundred troopers stood blocking the road, twice the number present on Bloody Sunday.

Dr. King asked for permission to pray, which was granted.

The marchers knelt, and Dr. King led them in prayer. As they stood back up, they were confronted by an incredible sight. The barricades had been pulled away and the troopers had stepped to the side of the road.

King was stunned.

Was it a trap? If Dr. King led the marchers forward, would he be leading them into a bloodbath? Were the troopers trying to humiliate him, undermine his leadership by offering a path he couldn't afford to take? Behind him two thousand marchers stirred, ready to move forward.

Dr. King suddenly wheeled around and shouted at them to go back. The marchers were confused. Dr. King shouted a second time for them to turn around, then walked back up the bridge. Andrew Young stood at the bottom of the bridge, motioning people to turn around.

Slowly, the marchers turned in a tight circle and walked back across the Edmund Pettus Bridge.

Emotions ran the gamut in the crowd of U-turning marchers. Many were euphoric that they hadn't been forced into the powerful blows of the troopers' nightsticks. Others felt betrayed, sure King's decision was a low point of moral courage for the whole civil rights movement.

Back at Brown Chapel, the crowd surged and floundered, filled with the energy to march and nowhere to go. Sheyann, relieved and excited there'd been no violence, slipped quickly between adults on the lawns of the Carver Homes, finding clergy from out of town, leading them by the hand to her apartment for a cup of coffee and a chance to sit down. One of the ministers, James Reeb, talked with her mother and promised he'd be back later for a cup of coffee after a meal in town at Walker's Café.

He never returned. Leaving the café with two other ministers, they were ambushed by four white men who clubbed Reeb in the head before vanishing into the darkness. Reeb was taken to the hospital in Birmingham, where he lay in a deep coma.

Dr. King stood on a razor's edge of self-doubt about his decision to turn the march around. He asked the out-of-towners to stay, sure the judge would grant them the right to march as soon as he reviewed the facts surrounding Bloody Sunday. Some disgusted out-of-towners left immediately, dubbing the march "Turn Around Tuesday,"

Protestors gathered on the wide, blocked-off street outside of Brown Chapel after the assult on James Reeb.
When it rained, they stood under makeshift shelters and tarps.

but others bunked down on floors in the Carver Homes and waited.

The next morning the mayor put up a wooden barrier across the street less than a block from the church and forbade all marching. Deputies, troopers, and Clark's posse backed him up. Protestors quickly dubbed it the "Berlin Wall" and hundreds of them kept up a constant vigil in the rain, singing freedom songs, chanting, and praying. On Thursday, March 11, Reeb died. More than a thousand kids cut school Friday and again Monday to stay out on the streets and protest.

On March 15, eight days after Bloody Sunday, protestors came in from their rain-soaked vigil to watch President Johnson address Congress in a live, televised broadcast. Dr. King and John Lewis had been invited to Washington, D.C., to hear the president speak in person, but decided to stay in Selma with other SCLC aides to watch on TV.

"I speak tonight for the dignity of man and the destiny of democracy," Johnson began, in a speech that had been written just minutes earlier.

"Rarely, in any time, does an issue lay bare the secret heart of America itself," he said. "The issue of equal rights for American Negroes is such an issue. . . . What happened in Selma is part of a far larger movement which reaches into every section and state of America. It is the effort of American Negroes to secure for themselves the full blessings of American life."

Listeners in Congress and across America were astonished. Johnson had just claimed Selma as a crucial battleground for civil rights, and thrown his full, public support behind it. Johnson went on to say that in two

days he would be sending to Congress "a law designed to eliminate illegal barriers to the right to vote." His speech was interrupted over and over again by applause.

"Their cause must be our cause too. It is not just Negroes, but all of us, who must overcome the crippling legacy of bigotry and injustice.

"And we shall overcome."

King's aides burst into cheers as the president evoked their anthem, the heart and soul of the civil rights movement, and adopted it as his own. Only Dr. King was silent. Lewis looked over at him and saw a tear slide down his cheek.

On Wednesday the federal judge officially issued his ruling on the right to march. When he compiled all the facts, he found an "almost continuous pattern . . . of harassment, intimidation, coercion, threatening conduct, and sometimes, brutal mistreatment" by state and local lawmen, "acting under the instructions of Governor Wallace." He granted Dr. King the right to lead a march from Selma to Montgomery.

The same day, President Johnson introduced a voting rights bill into Congress. With the federal government behind him, Dr. King immediately set a new march date: Sunday, March 21. And this time, they were going all the way to Montgomery.

Protestors often stood for hours with linked arms singing Freedom Songs while they waited for news of James Reeb's condition. These nuns came to Selma after seeing footage of Bloody Sunday. Joanne Blackmon is on the far right in the light coat, and Sheyann Webb is squeezed between two sisters.

DAY ONE

Sunday, March 21

Goal: David Hall's Farm

EXACTLY TWO WEEKS after Bloody Sunday, Dr. King led the procession from Brown Chapel. Religious leaders from across America walked beside him. Lynda's father had been adamant that she couldn't go all the way to Montgomery. He didn't want her to take such a big risk. But she had enlisted five respected, wise women who promised to watch out for her on the march, and he'd relented. She wanted Governor Wallace to see he hadn't hurt her spirit. "I wanted him to see my shaved head and I wanted him to see my face," she said, "'cuz it was still swollen and I still had bandages on it." Used to being away in jail, she packed extra underwear, shirts, and food. Charles and Bobby were enlisted as marshals for the whole march—to help get under way each day, assist those who needed it, and keep an eye out for trouble. Joanne, Sheyann, and Rachel were going for only the first day.

Near the front of the line was Cager Lee, the eighty-two-year-old grandfather of Jimmie Lee Jackson, whose death had sparked the march. "Yes, it was worth the boy dying," Cager Lee said. "He took me to church every Sunday, he worked hard. But he had to die for something. And thank God it was for this!"

Marchers flooded down Sylvan Street onto Alabama Avenue and made a wide turn onto Broad Street. The line kept swelling until three thousand people were streaming toward the Edmund Pettus Bridge in the early spring sunshine. Some carried suitcases and bedrolls.

Despite the joyful marchers' songs filling the air, organizers' nerves were strung tight. At a black church in nearby Birmingham, a ticking bomb made of forty-eight sticks of dynamite had been discovered, set to go off at noon. Demolition experts defused it, then rushed to disarm three more deadly bombs in town.

Above the line of marchers, two large military helicopters circled low, on the lookout for anything threatening. Governor Wallace had refused to provide protection, forcing President Johnson to federalize the Alabama National Guard, putting them under his control. For further safety, Johnson ordered 2,000 regular army troops to help guard the route.

Brisk winds swept over the marchers as they headed up and then down the arch of the Edmund Pettus Bridge. As they passed the site of Bloody Sunday and Turn Around Tuesday, they broke into cheers and singing.

Paul and Silas bound in jail
Had no money for da go de bail
Keep your eyes on the prize, hold on
Hold on, hold on
Keep your eyes on the prize, hold on

Songs rippled down the line of marchers. The line was so long, three or four songs could be sung at the same time without overlapping. In the adjacent lane, army jeeps, cars full of reporters, medical vans, water trucks, and flatbeds loaded with portable toilets drove slowly up and down the road.

"How could you ever think a day like this would come," said Cager Lee as he walked. He was marching for freedom in an area bound by the chains of slavery for his family. "My father was sold from Bedford, Va., into slavery down here. He'd tell how they sold slaves like they sold horse and mules. Have a man roll up his shirt sleeve and pants so they could see the muscles, you know."

At a rest stop seven miles out, Sheyann and Rachel saw Dr. King and rushed up to greet him. Buses were parked nearby, ready to take most of the marchers back to Selma. They had reached the point where Highway 80 narrowed from four lanes to two, and Dr. King had been

National Guardsmen, ordered by President Lyndon Johnson to protect the marchers, stand watch as the protestors leave Selma.

ordered to limit the march to three hundred people until the highway widened to four lanes again near Montgomery. A few of the teenagers who weren't chosen to keep going protested the twenty-two whites who got to continue marching. Andrew Young had to point out that including whites offered some protection against violence, and that it was meant to be an inclusive march.

Along with other tired marchers, Sheyann, Rachel, and Joanne clambered onto the buses for the ride back to Selma. Three hundred and eight marchers, most under twenty years old, and one-third female, turned off the highway onto a narrow country road leading to a farm. Four huge tents had been set up in the field. As evening fell, a large yellow rental truck drove up and unloaded shiny new metal garbage cans filled with dinner: spaghetti, pork and beans, and cornbread.

As soon as the sun disappeared, temperatures plummeted, and people headed into the tents. A generator growled in the background, fueling a few bare lightbulbs in each tent. Hissing kerosene heaters took the edge off the cold.

The students weren't ready to settle down. They stood three and four deep around a lead singer, singing and swaying through gospel and freedom songs. The leader suddenly shouted out, "One more time and really cool it." He sank down, lightly snapping his fingers.

Around him voices softened as people crouched, swaying, whisper-singing.

"Jump!" shouted the leader and everyone shot up into the air and shouted out and sang some more until the singing blended with laughter and quiet talk.

Outside, the National Guardsmen assigned to night duty lit small, crackling fires for warmth, making patches of yellow light in the dark. Inside, the heaters sputtered and ran out of kerosene. Bone-chilling fog crept in. There weren't enough blankets, coats, and sleeping bags to go around. Some people gave up trying to sleep and went outside, lit a fire in a trash barrel, and stood around it, shivering and talking quietly.

They were anxious about tomorrow, when they'd cross into Klan-infested Lowndes County. Instead of wide-open fields, they'd be walking through swamps and dense patches of woods. Most of the marchers lay in the tents, too tired to talk, too cold to sleep, listening as the students from Selma sang softly far into the night.

LEFT: John Lewis, far right, packed a few belongings into his knapsack. Twenty-year-old Doris Wilson carried hers in a waterproof bag under her arm. She'd been fired from her twelve-dollar-a-week job in a school lunchroom for taking part in the demonstrations. ABOVE: At the end of the day's walk, marchers sing freedom songs.

DAY TWO

Monday, March 22

Goal: Rosa Steele's Store

THE COLD, STIFF marchers were routed out of their tents early for the seventeen-mile trek to the next campsite. A heavy frost crackled under their feet as they shuffled forward in the chow line, where gluey oatmeal and watery coffee were being served out of the garbage cans.

As Lynda came out of the tent, she saw three National Guardsmen standing in front of a jeep, the butts of their guns perched on their waists, bayonets pointing up at the sky. She realized with a shock that they were just like the men who'd beaten her on the bridge. "It looked like they were staring straight at me," she said, as Bloody Sunday rushed back to her. "I thought they were there to kill me—to finish off the job they'd started." She started screaming.

Some people thought Lynda should be sent back to

Marchers walk under gathering storm clouds. A reconnaissance plane from the National Guard circles overhead, on the lookout for trouble.

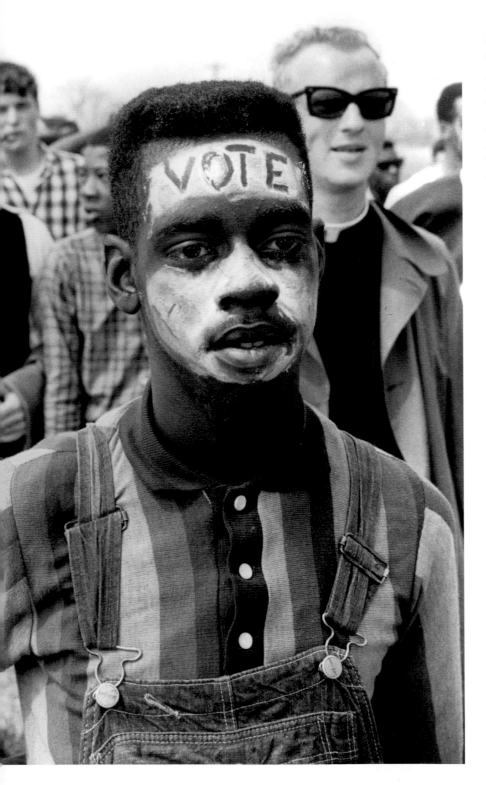

Selma, but the women looking out for her disagreed. They surrounded her, listening, soothing, talking. "They knew they couldn't send me back as scared as I was," Lynda said. "It would have destroyed me." A one-legged white man, Jim Letherer, told Lynda that before he'd let anyone hurt her, he'd lay down his life for her. She was astonished. "What kind of person would I be," she thought, "if I let him die for me?" Her determination rushed back. She was going all the way to Montgomery.

When the march crossed into Lowndes County, military protection increased. Eight new army jeeps went ahead of the marchers, along with a demolition team to check under the bridges for explosives. The helicopters circled protectively as the marchers entered the gloomy swamp, crossing Soapstone Creek safely, and then Big Swamp Creek. They sang their way past the draping Spanish moss, the murky water thick with mud and floating algae.

It was a relief when the swamp gave way to pastureland where small weathered shacks stood in the big fields, green grass pushing up through the stubble of last year's corn crop. Marchers shed sweaters and sweatshirts as the spring sun bounced off the asphalt. Soon they came to Trickem Fork, a cluster of houses with one church and a school. They'd made it nearly halfway to their goal: twenty miles from Brown Chapel, they had thirty more miles to go.

New rumors spread fast as they reached the end of day's march: a man had been spotted planting a bomb under a road bridge; twenty white men were seen prowling

Bobby Simmons used thick white sunscreen to write on his forehead.

through a nearby field, armed with guns. But the gossip was quickly squelched: it was just a boy who had hopped off his bike to relieve himself under the bridge; army demolition experts had been checking the area around the campsite.

As people ate dinner and settled down for a second night on the ground, the medical team busily treated exhausted marchers with blistered feet. Dr. King gave a short press conference, and everyone readied themselves for another cold, damp night.

At midnight, Charles was woken up by a frightened teenager who'd slipped into the tent. He was thinking about starting a youth movement in his high school and wanted to know what motivated Charles. "You really believe in non-violence?" the boy asked Charles.

"I do," Charles said. "I used to think of it as just a tactic, but now I believe in it all the way." He wasn't worried about more violence for his own sake. It would only be a test of his commitment. "It's easy to talk about non-violence," he said, "but in a lot of cases you've got to be tested, and re-inspire yourself." His only concern was for the others from Hudson High School, making sure they were all safe.

By 2 A.M. everyone in the campsite was asleep except for the night guards and two shortwave radio operators in a truck. They were in constant touch with Selma, where busloads of people were still pouring into town.

The marchers camped on Rosa Steele's property, near her small general store. Asked if she was worried about retaliation from local whites, Mrs. Steele replied, "I'm not afraid. I've lived my three score and ten."

DAY THREE

Tuesday, March 23

Goal: A. G. Gaston's Pasture

THE MARCHERS WOKE up to a drizzling rain. Folksinger Len Chandler cut a hole in the middle of a starry towel he'd brought and put it on as a patriotic vest. He pulled two pairs of socks onto his blistered feet and stuffed an extra pair in his guitar case.

The drizzle had turned into a downpour by 10:30. Huge raindrops pummeled them, hitting the crushed gravel and dust and splattering gritty mud up to their knees. The jeeps and trucks turned their windshield wipers and headlights on. "Free-dom! Free-dom! Free-dom!"

chanted dozens of marchers. After standing up to Sherriff Clark and his jails, they weren't about to let a little rain stop them.

The weather cleared up by the time the soaked marchers arrived at the tents set up on high ground near the junction of Route 80 and Route 21. But relief that the day's march was over was brief. The campsite was a muddy mess. Straw was thrown down to cover the mud, but it was soon pushed into the muck. A few weary, cold people called it quits, and were driven back to Selma.

Plastic sheeting went down on the oozing ground as people staked out spots for the night. Tempers flared. Most people were desperate for sleep, but the high schoolers were still full of laughter and songs after everyone turned in. An exhausted white Northerner finally stood up and yelled, "You goddamn kids, shut up!"

The students sang back softly that they'd "Cool it when the spirit say cool it."

LEFT: *Doris Wilson refused to let the weather dampen her spirit. "I'm marching for my freedom," she said.*
BELOW: *Heavy rains left the campsite wet and soggy.*

DAY FOUR

Wednesday, March 24

Goal: City of Saint Jude

DESPITE ANOTHER BREAKFAST of weak coffee and pasty oatmeal, the marchers set off cheerfully. Tonight they'd been promised entertainment. Then they'd sleep on the ground for the last time, get up, and march to the state capitol building.

Chandler borrowed a fife and began playing tunes, the piercing, martial notes traveling up and down the line of marchers. Students started a round of "Yankee Doodle" and quickly turned it into a freedom song.

> *Wallace said we couldn't march*
> *We knew he was a phony*
> *Now we're marching all the way*
> *To make him eat baloney*

Martin Luther King Jr. and his wife, Coretta Scott King, march and sing with the Abernathy kids. On the far left in a fur hat is their father, Ralph Abernathy.

As soon as the marchers moved out of Lowndes County, word was sent back to Selma. Everyone was welcome to join them now. Hundreds of people waiting on the grounds of the Carver Homes sped toward them. Joanne found a ride and came looking for her sister. Dr. King, who'd left the march for a day to give a speech, rejoined with his wife, Coretta Scott King.

Cars and buses pulled over to the side of the road, and people spilled out to join the line. By late afternoon, five thousand clean, energetic people had joined the three hundred muddy, exultant marchers. They inundated the last campsite, the City of Saint Jude, a Catholic compound of red-brick buildings on the outskirts of Montgomery.

Lynda walked into St. Jude, dropped down on the grass, and began crying. She couldn't stop. She'd made it. "All that fear, all that pain, the anger that had driven me there that stemmed from Bloody Sunday was finally released," she said. "I was in Montgomery."

Three hundred orange vests were handed out to the stalwart marchers who'd walked the whole fifty-four miles. It dawned on Bobby what an honor it was to be given one. He'd been jailed more times than he could count. He'd walked every step of the way from Selma. These were more than just safety vests. Students quickly renamed them "orange badges."

The tents had been set up in the big field behind the buildings. When darkness fell, the generator stalled, providing only enough power to light a makeshift stage set up at one end of a tent. The excited crowd surrounded the stage, sang along with folksingers, and howled in laugher at comedians.

Coretta Scott King was talked into making a rare speech. Struggling through the tightly packed bodies, she was lifted up onto the platform. Right now, she said, they were just eighty miles from where she had been raised near Marion, picking cotton on her family farm. She'd grown up with Jimmie Lee Jackson's family, and his death had hit her hard. But marching with everyone, she wasn't afraid, not even when they'd walked through Lowndes County. She finished with a favorite poem by Langston Hughes:

MOTHER TO SON

Well, son, I'll tell you:
Life for me ain't been no crystal stair.
It's had tacks in it,
And splinters,
And boards torn up,

And places with no carpet on the floor—
Bare.
But all the time
I'se been a-climbin' on,
And reachin' landin's,
And turnin' corners,
And sometimes goin' in the dark
Where there ain't been no light.
So boy, don't you turn back.
Don't you set down on the steps
'Cause you finds it's kinder hard.
Don't you fall now—
For I'se still goin', honey,
I'se still climbin',
And life for me ain't been no crystal stair.

Joanne looked everywhere for Lynda, but in the crush of people she couldn't find her sister. As she searched, she kept running into women from Montgomery walking through the crowd saying, "I'se cooked a huge meal. Come home with me." Joanne and two of her friends went to a woman's house to eat dinner and spend the night. Lynda was invited to another. After dinner and a bath, she fell into a deep sleep. Charles and Bobby happily toughed it out in the dark, muddy tents.

Len Chandler plays the fife to keep people's spirits up, next to one-legged Jim Letherer, who stoically made the entire walk on crutches.

DAY FIVE

Thursday, March 25

Goal: Capitol Building in Montgomery

THIS TIME THERE was a send-off breakfast of eggs, creamy grits, and fried chicken made by a crew of churchwomen. As the well-fed marchers set out in a misty rain, people rushed in to join them at every intersection. They'd come to Montgomery from all over the United States, by car and plane, train and bus. Rosa Parks flew down from Detroit, Michigan, back to the city where she'd refused to give up her seat on the bus in 1955. Sheyann and her parents drove from Selma, and Lynda and Joanne's father brought a carful.

The march swelled to 30,000. Streaming up Mobile Street to Montgomery Street, they eased around the fountain at Court Square, where Parks had boarded her bus. Up the six broad blocks of Dexter Avenue—known as Goat Hill—they surged.

In their orange vests and mud-caked shoes, Bobby and Charles were sent forward along with other students

Marchers fill the street in downtown Montgomery. Rosa Parks, toward the center front in a light dress and dark hat, walks next to Ralph Abernathy.

as an honor vanguard. Charles, his vest over his Hudson High sweatshirt, strutted joyfully up front. "Come and march with us," he urged bystanders, black and white, through a megaphone. "We're going downtown. There's nothing to be afraid of. Come and march with us!" He turned around and looked down Goat Hill at the thousands and thousands of people walking behind him. "It was just such a glorious triumph," he said.

Folksingers jumped up on a makeshift stage next to the capitol building. Patriotic songs blended into gospel and protest songs. "The Star-Spangled Banner" rolled into "Go Tell It on the Mountain" and "This Land Is Your Land" as the singers harmonized. Speaker after speaker addressed the crowd.

It was no surprise that Governor Wallace didn't show up. Marchers were sure he was in his office high up in the state capitol, peeking down at them through the closed curtains. "I had some satisfaction that he was scared of me," Lynda said. "I didn't do anything to that big old man."

Bobby, a few feet from the stage, was euphoric. "You be rejoicing once you accomplish your goal and get there," he said. "I never seen so many people. It was just people galore. As far as you could see back by eyes there were people, just standing, and nobody seemed to get tired."

Rosa Parks was coaxed up on the stage and greeted with a roar of delight.

In her soft voice, she told the crowd about her childhood memories of sitting next to her grandfather, a shot-gun across his lap, as the Klan rode by on the gravel road in front of their house. She spoke briefly and then stepped away from the microphones.

Finally it was time for Dr. King. He spoke of the long, dark legacy of slavery and segregation, the triumphs of the civil rights movement, the hardships ahead. He urged—begged—everyone to remain committed to nonviolence as they built "a society at peace with itself."

Today I want to tell the city of Selma, today I want to say to the state of Alabama, today I want to say to the people of America and the nations of the world, that we are not about to turn around. We are on the move now. . . . Like an idea whose time has come, not even the marching of mighty armies can halt us. We are moving to the land of freedom.

I come to say to you this afternoon, however difficult the moment, however frustrating the hour, it will not be long, because "truth crushed to earth will rise again."

How long? Not long, because "no lie can live forever."

How long? Not long, because "you shall reap what you sow."

How long? Not long, because the arc of the moral universe is long, but it bends toward justice.

RIGHT: Rosa Parks addresses the crowd. OVERLEAF: A sea of flags and marchers, seen from the impromptu stage.

54 • Elizabeth Partridge

King finished by reciting one of his favorite song choruses, his rich preacher's voice rolling out over the crowd:

Glory, hallelujah! His truth is
marching on!

The speeches were over. The hot days and hard pavement, the cold nights, the rain and mud were done. The defiance and exhilaration were falling away. But before they left, thirty thousand people clasped hands, swaying back and forth as they sang.

We shall overcome
We shall overcome
We shall overcome some day

Oh, deep in my heart I do believe
We shall overcome some day

People were urged to go quietly and be off the streets before dark. Victory and jubilation turned to a sudden feeling of vulnerability. Cars full of marchers hurried back to Selma. Word spread quickly when a white woman, Viola Liuzzo, was gunned down and killed by Klan members as she drove to Montgomery to pick up marchers.

"When we returned back to Selma, we returned under a cloud of sadness," Lynda said. "I didn't return jubilant." As cars pulled up in front of Brown Chapel people were rushed inside. No one knew if gunmen lurked outside, ready to strike again.

ABOVE: John Lewis, wearing his vest, speaks to the crowd. RIGHT: After signing the
Voting Rights Act into law, President Johnson hands one of the signing pens
to Dr. King, watched by Ralph Abernathy, August 6, 1965.

VOTING RIGHTS ACT

August 6, 1965

IN WASHINGTON D.C., President Johnson moved quickly. He used both the triumph and tragedy of the march to insist that Congress work together and hammer out a voting rights law. On August 6, 1965, the Voting Rights Act was ready for him to sign. It outlawed literacy tests and poll taxes and authorized the Attorney General to appoint federal registrars, if necessary, to make sure all qualified citizens were free to register. Dr. King and Rosa Parks were among those chosen to witness the historic bill's signing.

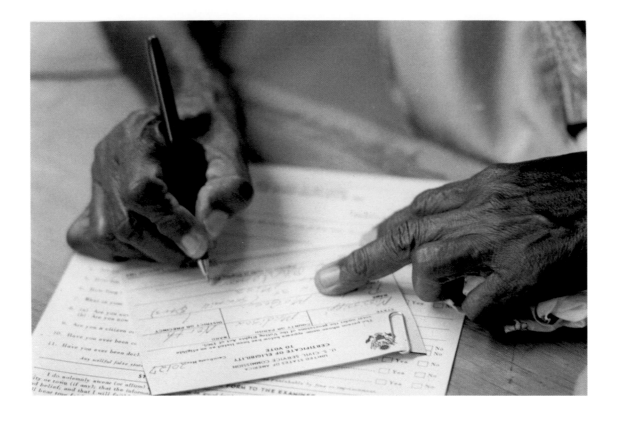

President Johnson ordered federal registrars to start immediately. On August 10, 1965, Charles's mother, Ardies Mauldin, became the first person in the United States to register under the Voting Rights Act. By the end of the day, more than one hundred new black voters had been added in Dallas County. In Perry County, Cager Lee registered to vote for the first time in his life. In less than a year, Dallas County added more than 8,500 new black registrants to the voting rolls. All across the South, people stood in long lines to register. This time they weren't turned away with cattle prods and billy clubs.

Selma, Dr. King said, was a "shining moment."

It was also a testimony to nonviolent protest. Hundreds of students had put themselves at risk to change America's voting laws. Their idealism and bravery encouraged the adults. Together, they learned to live with fear, but did not let it stop them. With only their songs and faith for protection, they believed they could make a difference.

And they did.

Throughout the South, the presence of federal registrars ensured that all citizens could register to vote. Above, an applicant registers in Canton, Mississppi, 1965.

AUTHOR'S NOTE

THERE ARE MOMENTS in history that grab me tight and don't let go. When I came across Matt Herron's photos of the Selma-Montgomery march at www.takestockphotos.com, shivers chased up and down my spine. I headed for the library. After reading through a stack of books, I was totally and completely hooked. The march is loaded with so many rich themes: the brilliant strategies Dr. King employed, his devotion to civil rights, the backstage alliance between Dr. King and President Johnson. I wanted to know more about what led up to the combustion in Selma: the incredibly complex history of slavery, Jim Crow, and crippling legislation.

I found the story of the march has often been told from the viewpoint of important civil rights activists like Dr. King, Andrew Young, and John Lewis. But as Lewis acknowledged, Selma was not like the other movements, with leaders planning every move. "Selma was more of a bottom-up campaign," said Lewis. "We were there to guide and help carry out what the people wanted to do, but it was essentially the people themselves who pointed the way."

What people?

Women like Amelia Boynton and Mrs. Johnson. But the adults couldn't do it alone. It took hundreds of kids and young adults who walked right into jail, into billy clubs and cattle prods, over and over again. Their individual acts of determination and bravery, added together, left an indelible mark on America.

I'd found the story I wanted to tell: how these kids changed history. I was awed by their commitment to nonviolence, to meeting brutality and hatred with love. I wanted to understand how simple, easy-to-remember songs helped them to be so courageous. I wondered . . . would I have been that brave?

I went to Selma, Alabama, to interview people who'd been kids and young adults during the movement. They'd grown up, married, had children, worked, gone to school, moved away, returned to Selma. I asked them to take me back to 1965. I wanted to hear about their families, school, being in jail, their favorite songs. They all spoke of Bloody Sunday as the most terrifying day of their lives, and walking into Montgomery as one of the most ecstatic. In recent years they'd become aware of the devastating price they'd paid for being out there, vulnerable, day after day. "There's a lot of pain in all of us that never came out," said Charles Mauldin when I interviewed him. Joanne Blackmon Bland agreed. "You don't realize how damaged you are."

But they didn't waste any time feeling sorry for them-

selves. What stirred them all were the changes that had come and continue to come. "It's the good times that make you cry," Charles told me. "Not the bad times. You've seen something be accomplished and it really is heart-rending." They also considered their involvement in Selma as part of a bigger picture. In an interview with the National Park Service, Joanne Blackmon Bland said, "They like to say these particular struggles were black struggles, but they were not. . . . We fought this movement primarily because it benefited us as a whole. But if you look at the pictures and read about the history of it, it was not a black movement—it was a people movement. And the future has to be a people movement, until injustice is stamped out in any form."

And we do it with the great democratic tradition: voting. So simple. So powerful.

The "Berlin Wall," first a wooden barricade, was replaced by a thin rope. The barrier was removed after James Reeb's death.
LEFT: A boy victoriously holds up a small section of the rope. RIGHT: Singing behind the Berlin Wall.

SOURCE NOTES

VOTELESS, 1963

"A vote-less people . . .": Robinson, *Bridge Across Jordan*, 225.

"Fear is the key . . .": Woffurd, *Of Kennedys and Kings*, 112.

"If we in the South . . .": Lewis, *Walking with the Wind*, 180.

"Segregation now, segregation tomorrow . . .": McCabe and Stekler, *The American Experience*, "George Wallace."

MARTIN LUTHER KING JR. ARRIVES, 1965
January 2

"This little light . . .": *Freedom Songs*, liner notes, 4.

"a symbol of bitter-end resistance . . .": Kotz, *Judgment Days*, 254.

lighting a fire . . .: National Park Service, "Selma to Montgomery National Historic Trail," Lowery.

January 4–14

"If you can't vote . . .": Webb and Nelson, *Selma, Lord, Selma*, 11.

"Don't worry about your children . . .": *Sing for Freedom*, cut 20.

"Why do you have to drink . . .": Mauldin, personal interview.

"I always had an answer . . .": National Park Service, "Selma to Montgomery National Historic Trail," Mauldin.

"From a child up . . ." "They had a lot of fear . . ." and "Please leave that mess . . .": Simmons, personal interview.

Up until World War II . . . : Blackmon, *Slavery by Another Name*, 65, 379.

"The movement was like . . .": National Park Service, "Selma to Montgomery National Historic Trail," Lowery.

January 18–22

Rachel got home . . .: Webb and Nelson, *Selma, Lord, Selma*, 24.

"Now, you're going across the line . . ." and "Mr. White Man . . .": Hampton and Fayer, *Voices of Freedom*, 211–12.

"Baby, don't be afraid . . .": Hampton and Fayer, *Voices of Freedom*, 219.

"If *death* was the option . . ." "That song was . . ." and "Not that any of us . . .": Bonner, personal interview.

"Oh Freedom . . .": *Freedom Songs*, liner notes, 2.

"They treated you . . ." and "After the first time . . .": Simmons, personal interview.

February 1–17

"Even though they cannot vote . . .": Branch, *Pillar of Fire*, 575.

"We're gonna do . . .": *WNEW's Story of Selma*, liner notes, 5.

"We want to make them . . ." and "All of you underage . . .": Herbers, "Negros Step Up Drive in Alabama."

"We had to sleep . . ." and "I'll be right there . . .": Watters, "Why the Negro Children March."

"A hundred times . . .": King, Martin Luther, Jr., *The Words of Martin Luther King, Jr.*, 54.

"If you miss Governor Wallace . . .": *Voices of the Civil Rights Movement*, disc 1, cut 3.

"You've been wanting to march . . .": Kotz, *Judgment Days*, 274.

"God sees you . . ." and "You'd be beat . . .": Watters, "Why the Negro Children March."

"You have to cut yourself off . . .": Mauldin, personal interview.

"I'm proud of you . . .": Watters, "Why the Negro Children March."

"The adults that came . . .": Bland, personal interview.

"If you cannot sing . . .": Seeger and Reiser, *Everybody Says Freedom*, 82.

"And for God's sake . . .": Lowery, personal interview.

February 19–March 6, 1965

"Be prepared to walk . . .": Branch, *At Canaan's Edge*, 9.

BLOODY SUNDAY: MARCH 7, 1965

"Tear gas will . . .": Carson, *Reporting Civil Rights Part Two*, 336.

"We were going to get killed . . .": Seeger and Reiser, *Everybody Says Freedom*, 191.

"There's a type of coolness . . .": National Park Service, "Selma to Montgomery National Historic Trail," Mauldin.

"Go home or go . . .": Branch, *At Canaan's Edge*, 50.

"This is it . . .": Lewis, *Walking with the Wind*, 328.

"People were laying out . . .": Simmons, personal interview.

"They ran those horses . . .": "Joanne Bland," *Baylor Magazine*.

"They would lean over . . .": Simmons, personal interview.

"It was pure hatred . . .": Lowery, personal interview.

"You ever see . . .": Hampton, *Eyes on the Prize*.

"like we were slaves . . .": Webb and Nelson, *Selma, Lord, Selma*, 105.

TURN AROUND TUESDAY: MARCH 9

"Mine eyes have seen . . .": Boni, *Fireside Book of Favorite American Songs*, 145.

"Thank God we're . . .": Webb and Nelson, *Selma, Lord, Selma*, 109.

"We must let them know . . .": Branch, *At Canaan's Edge*, 64.

"Mr. Attorney General . . .": Kotz, *Judgment Days*, 292.

"I do not know . . .": Kotz, *Judgment Days*, 295.

"I held Lynda's hand . . ." and "If you don't go . . .": National Park Service, "Selma to Montgomery National Historic Trail," Bland.

"I speak tonight . . ." "Rarely, in any time . . ." "a law designed to eliminate . . ." and "Their cause must be . . .": www.cspan.org/PresidentialLibraries/Content/LBJ/LBJ_VotingRights.pdf

"almost continuous pattern . . .": Kotz, *Judgment Days*, 316.

DAY ONE: SUNDAY, MARCH 21

"I wanted him to see . . .": National Park Service, "Selma to Montgomery National Historic Trail," Lowery.

"Yes, it was worth the boy . . .": Kotz, *Judgment Days*, 320.

"How could you ever think . . .": Carson, *Reporting Civil Rights Part Two*, 354.

"One more time . . ." and "Jump!": Chandler, "Selma: A Folksinger's Report," 10.

DAY TWO: MONDAY, MARCH 22

"It looked like . . ." "They knew they couldn't send . . ." and "What kind of person . . .": Lowery, personal interview.

"You really believe . . ." "I do . . ." and "It's easy to talk . . .": Adler, "Letter from Selma."

"I'm not afraid . . .": "National Report," 47.

DAY THREE: TUESDAY, MARCH 23

"You goddamn kids . . ." and "Cool it when . . .": Wofford, *Of Kennedys and Kings*, 194.

DAY FOUR: WEDNESDAY, MARCH 24

"Wallace said we couldn't march . . .": WNEW's *Story of Selma*, liner notes, 3.

"All that fear . . .": National Park Service, "Selma to Montgomery National Historic Trail," Lowery.

She'd grown up . . .: Wofford, *Of Kennedys and Kings* 190.

"Mother to Son . . .": Hughes, *Collected Poems*, 30.

"I'se cooked a huge meal . . .": Bland, personal interview.

DAY FIVE: THURSDAY, MARCH 25

"Come and march . . .": Adler, "Letter from Selma."

"It was such . . .": National Park Service, "Selma to Montgomery National Historic Trail," Mauldin.

"I had some satisfaction . . .": Lowery, personal interview.

"You be rejoicing . . .": Simmons, personal interview.

"Today I want to tell . . ." and "Glory, hallelujah! . . .": http://stanford.edu/group/King/publications/speeches/Our_God_is_marching_on.html

"When we returned . . .": National Park Service, "Selma to Montgomery National Historic Trail," Lowery.

VOTING RIGHTS ACT: AUGUST 6, 1965

By the end of the day . . .: Garrow, *Protest at Selma*, 181.

In less than a year . . .: Garrow, *Protest at Selma*, 187.

"a shining moment": Kotz, *Judgment Days*, 337.

AUTHOR'S NOTE

"Selma was more . . .": Lewis, *Walking with the Wind*, 307.

"There's a lot of pain . . .": Mauldin, personal interview.

"You don't realize . . .": Bland, personal interview.

"It's the good times . . .": Mauldin, personal interview.

"They like to say . . .": National Park Service, "Selma to Montgomery National Historic Trail," Bland.

BIBLIOGRAPHY

Articles, Films, Interviews, Music, and Online Sources

Adler, Renata. "Letter from Selma," *The New Yorker*, April 10, 1965. http://www.newyorker.com/archive/1965/04/10/1965_04_10_121_TNY_CARDS_000282138

Bland, Joanne Blackmon. Personal interview with author, November 5, 2008.

Bonner, Charles. Personal interview with author, December 11, 2008.

Chandler, Len, Jr. "Selma: A Folksinger's Report." *Sing Out!*, volume 15, number 3, July 1965.

Freedom Songs: Selma, Alabama. Smithsonian Folkways Recordings, 1965.

Hampton, Henry, executive producer. *Eyes on the Prize: America's Civil Rights Years 1954–1964*. Episode 6, "Bridge to Freedom: 1965." Blackside, Inc., 1987.

Herbers, John. "Negros Step Up Drive in Alabama: 1,000 More Seized." *New York Times*, February 4, 1965.

"Joanne Bland." *Baylor Magazine*, volume 2, number 2, Sept./Oct. 2003. http://www.baylormag.com/story.php?story=004479

Lowery, Lynda Blackmon. Personal interview with author, November 5, 2008.

Mauldin, Charles. Personal interview with author, November 6, 2008.

Mccabe, Daniel, and Paul Stekler, producers and directors. "George Wallace: Settin' the Woods on Fire," *The American Experience*, 2000. http://www.pbs.org/wgbh/amex/wallace/filmmore/transcript/index.html

National Park Service. "Selma to Montgomery National Historic Trail: People of the Movement." Bland, Joanne. http://www.nps.gov/hfc/av/semo/docs/ (click on NPSSM-33—Anderson, Bland)

_____. "Selma to Montgomery National Historic Trail: People of the Movement." Lowery, Lynda. http://www.nps.gov/hfc/av/semo/docs/ (click on NPSSM-50—Lowery)

_____. "Selma to Montgomery National Historic Trail: People of the Movement." Mauldin, Charles. http://www.nps.gov/hfc/av/semo/docs/ (click on NPSSM-07 John Jackson, Charles Mauldin, Zannie Murphy)

"National Report," *Jet*, volume 27, number 26, April 8, 1965.

Simmons, Bobby. Personal interview with author, November 5, 2008.

Sing for Freedom: The Story of the Civil Rights Movement Through Its Songs. Smithsonian Folkways Recordings, 1990.

Voices of the Civil Rights Movement: Black American Freedom Songs 1960–1966. Smithsonian Folkways Recordings, 1997.

Watters, Pat. "Why the Negro Children March," *New York Times*, March 21, 1965.

WNEW'S Story of Selma with Len Chandler, Pete Seeger and the Freedom Voices. Smithsonian Folkways Recordings, 1965.

Books

Blackmon, Douglas A. *Slavery by Another Name: The Re-Enslavement of Black Americans from the Civil War to World War II*. New York: Doubleday, 2008.

Boni, Margaret Bradford. *The Fireside Book of Favorite American Songs*. New York: Simon and Schuster, 1952.

Branch, Taylor. *At Canaan's Edge: America in the King Years 1965–68*. New York: Simon and Schuster, 2006.

_____. *Pillar of Fire: America in the King Years 1963–65*. New York: Simon and Schuster, 1998.

Carson, Clayborne, editor. *Reporting Civil Rights Part Two: American Journalism 1963–1973*. New York: Library of America, 2003.

Chester, J. L. , with Julia Cass. *Black in Selma*. New York: Farrar, Straus and Giroux, 1990.

Durham, Michael S. *Powerful Days: The Civil Rights Photography of Charles Moore*. Tuscaloosa: University of Alabama Press, published in cooperation with the Birmingham Civil Rights Institute, 2002.

Fager, Charles. *Selma, 1965*. New York: Charles Scribner's Sons, 1974.

Garrow, David. *Protest at Selma: Martin Luther King, Jr., and the Voting Rights Act of 1965*. New Haven: Yale University Press, 1978.

Hampton, Henry, and Steve Fayer. *Voices of Freedom: An Oral History of the Civil Rights Movement from the 1950s through the 1980s*. New York: Bantam Books, 1990.

Hughes, Langston. *The Collected Poems of Langston Hughes*. Edited by Arnold Rampersad. New York: Knopf, 1994.

King, Martin Luther, Jr. *A Call to Conscience: The Landmark Speeches of Martin Luther King, Jr.* Edited by Clayborne Carson and Kris Shepard. New York: IPM/Warner Books, 2001.

King, Martin Luther, Jr. *The Words of Martin Luther King, Jr.* Selected and introduced by Coretta Scott King. New York: Newmarket Press, 1987.

_____, and Clayborne Carson. *The Autobiography of Martin Luther King Jr.* New York: Intellectual Properties Management, Inc. in association with Warner Books, 1998.

Kotz, Nick. *Judgment Days: Lyndon Baines Johnson, Martin Luther King Jr., and the Laws That Changed America*. New York: Houghton Mifflin Company, 2005.

Lewis, John. *Walking with the Wind: A Memoir of the Movement*. New York: Simon and Schuster, 1998.

Robinson, Amelia Boynton. *Bridge Across Jordan*. Revised edition. Washington D.C.: Schiller Institute, 1991.

Seeger, Pete, and Bob Reiser. *Everybody Says Freedom: A History of the Civil Rights Movement in Songs and Pictures*. New York: W. W. Norton, 1989.

Webb, Sheyann, and Rachel West Nelson, as told to Frank Sikora. *Selma, Lord, Selma: Girlhood Memories of the Civil-Rights Days*. Tuscaloosa: University of Alabama Press, 1980.

Wofford, Harris. *Of Kennedys and Kings: Making Sense of the Sixties*. New York: Farrar, Straus and Giroux, 1980.

Young, Andrew. *An Easy Burden: The Civil Rights Movement and the Transformation of America*. New York: Harper Collins, 1996.

Resources: More Reading, Listening, Looking, Browsing

Additional resources for the Selma to Montgomery march are amazingly varied and plentiful.

Would you like to hear Sheyann and Rachel sing "This Little Light of Mine" outside Brown Chapel? How about Hudson High School student Bettie Mae Fikes's powerful rendition of the same song, recorded at a student meeting?

Maybe you'd like to do more reading, see more photos, rent a video, take a virtual tour of the march, or plan a real-time visit. Perhaps you'd like to listen to a taped conversation between Dr. King and President Johnson, or watch interviews with other people who were involved in Selma, 1965.

If you're wondering about the long-term reverberations of the march in today's America, you can watch footage of President Barack Obama's visit to Selma, or listen to his moving March 18, 2008, speech on race. You can read about Representative John Lewis, who has served in Congress since 1986, and about Andrew Young's rich, varied life in politics. Maybe you're curious about the kids—now adults—whose stories, woven together, are this book.

Check out all these connections on my Web site:
www.elizabethpartridge.com.

PERMISSIONS: *Photo Credits*

Wind billows the flag around teen protestor Lewis "Big June" Marshall on the march into Montgomery, March 1965.

Quotations

"Mother to Son," from *The Collected Poems of Langston Hughes*, by Langston Hughes, edited by Arnold Rampersad with David Roessel, Associate Editor. © 1994 by the Estate of Langston Hughes. Used by permission of Alfred A. Knopf, a division of Random House Inc.

Quotations by Dr. Martin Luther King Jr. are reprinted by arrangement with The Heirs to the Estate of Martin Luther King Jr., c/o Writers House as agent for the proprietor. New York, N.Y. © 1963 Dr. Martin Luther King Jr.; copyright renewed 1991 Coretta Scott King.

Lyrics

"Ain't Gonna Let Nobody Turn Me 'Round": Arrangement by Bernice Johnson Reagon. Copyright © 2000 Songtalk Publishing Co., Washington, D.C. Used by Permission.

"Eyes on the Prize (Hold On)": Arrangement by Bernice Johnson Reagon. Copyright © 2000 Songtalk Publishing Co., Washington, D.C. Used by Permission.

"If You Miss Me from the Back of the Bus": Original lyrics by Charles Neblett. Selma-inspired lyrics by Bettie Mae Fikes. Used with permission of Charles Neblett and Bettie Mae Fikes.

"We Shall Overcome": Musical and Lyrical adaptation by Zilphia Horton, Frank Hamilton, Guy Carawan, and Pete Seeger. Inspired by African American Gospel Singing, members of the Food & Tobacco Workers Union, Charleston, S.C., and the southern Civil Rights Movement. TRO-Copyright © 1960 (Renewed) and 1963 (Renewed) Ludlow Music, Inc., New York, N.Y. Royalties derived from this composition are being contributed to the We Shall Overcome Fund and The Freedom Movement under the Trusteeship of the writers. Used by Permission.

"Yankee Doodle (Wallace Said We Couldn't March)": Lyrics by Len Chandler. Used with permission of Len Chandler.

ACKNOWLEDGMENTS

TO THE PEOPLE who opened their hearts to me, shared their memories, relived the terror of Bloody Sunday and the exhilaration of marching into Montgomery. This is your book, and I thank you from the bottom of my heart: Joanne Blackmon Bland, Charles Bonner, Lynda Blackmon Lowery, Charles Mauldin, and Bobby Simmons. Thank you also to Frank Sikora, Sheyann Webb, and Rachel West Nelson. Sikora's interviews of Sheyann and Rachel as teens resulted in the book *Selma, Lord, Selma: Girlhood Memories of the Civil Rights Days*. It's still in print, and a wonderful read. Many thanks to Rachel for responding to my questions in a letter. A special shout-out to Charles Mauldin, who helped identify many of the students caught by photographers but rarely named.

My deep gratitude to photographer Matt Herron for jumpstarting this book; John F. Phillips, who culled through his images to find just the perfect ones; Julian Cox, curator of photography at the High Museum in Atlanta; and Andrew Schneider at the Martin Luther King, Jr., Research and Education Institute.

Grateful thanks to the writers and illustrators who encouraged me: Susan Campbell Bartoletti, Laurie Halse Anderson, Gary and Anna Grossnickle Hines, the Wu Li gang, and my posse: Judy Blundell, Julie Downing, and Katherine Tillotson. To the Viking team: publisher Regina Hayes who kept the faith, my gracious editor Catherine Frank, brilliant designer Jim Hoover, and the incomparable Janet Pascal. To friends and family who pulled me back to the twenty-first century when I wandered too long in 1965: my husband, Tom Ratcliff, our sons, Felix and Will, and their wonderful girlfriends, Sasha Harris-Lovett and Nicolette Zeliadt; my friends Clair Brown, Syd Feeney, Karen Kashkin, and Andrea Nachtigall. Special thanks to my sister Meg, who drew out timelines for me and kept me to them in her kind and serious way, and my sister Joan, who lightened my load.

INDEX

Numbers in **boldface** refer to illustrations.